1000 FACTS & KNOWLEDGE FOR CURIOUS KIDS

1000 Facts & Knowledge for Curious Kids

Fascinating and True Facts About History, Science, Space, Geography and Pop Culture the Whole Family Will Love

by Henry Bennett

Liberstax Publishing

GET TWO BONUS BOOKS FOR FREE!

To help you along your investing in knowledge journey, we've provided a free and exclusive copy of the short book, *Amazing Quick-Fire Facts,* and a bonus copy of book, *The Big Book of Fun Riddles & Jokes.*

We highly recommend you sign up now to get the most out of these books. You can do that by visiting https://www.subscribepage.com/henrybennett to receive your FREE copies!

REVIEW PLEASE?

WE WOULD REALLY
APPRECIATE YOUR
REVIEW ON AMAZON!

To leave an Amazon review please visit
https://www.amazon.com/ryp or scan the QR code below...

Contents

Introduction

When you think of our planet it's impossible to process how big it is, and we often get overloaded with information. But this book will introduce you in a simple and fun way to learn some of the most unusual, surprising, and downright fantastic facts about the Earth.

Do you like to read about new things that make you scratch your head in disbelief? Well, this book is a collection of facts and trivia for children and teenagers of all ages. You can read them yourself, enjoy the illustrations and you'll be equipped to share what you've learned to your friends and family. There is also plenty of family fun to be had too—you can read the facts together or turn it into a quiz, we guarantee that adults and grandparents will be learning some astonishing new trivia as well.

Would you like to find out which famous holiday destination used to be called the Sandwich Islands? Do you know what is considered the hardest material in the world? Let's find out where pizza originated from? Can you believe there were once giant penguins? Have you ever wondered what the ozone layer protects Earth from? Why do water bottles have an expiry date if water doesn't expire? Who was the first Roman to invade

Great Britain? The book will leave you thinking that's strange but it's all completely true!

You will read about some of the craziest, funniest, and most unbelievable facts in the known to humans, but you can be assured that each piece of information is 100% factual.

Adventure back through the history books as we discover lots of facts about the people, places, and happenings. Experience with us as we retell historical moments, wonder at the kings and queens of old, the geniuses who discovered medicines and who built the Empire State Building in New York. Read interesting snippets about animals and the largest sharks that ever lived. Find out some strange sleeping habits of the Ancient Egyptians and where the word "quarantine" comes from.

It is organised into 13 chapters mostly by subject including– science, history, geography, space, pop culture, food and health, inventions and discoveries, and a general melting pot of everything, so there's sure to be something for everyone here. The arrangement of this book is what makes it so unique and entertaining. You can pick and choose a chapter, or a selection of facts, and move around the book, back and forth.

You are guaranteed to enjoy reading this book, even the chapters or subjects that may not normally interest you. This isn't your everyday long-winded history, science, or mathematics book, full of boring information, dry language, and a lot of repetitive gibberish that is hard to follow. Not at all, this book is written in a way that you'll learn bitesize facts with simple explanations that will stick in your mind for you to retrieve them when the future calls.

If you need an easy conversation starter when you meet someone new, or if you want to surprise your friends what you've learned about the world, or you want to take it with you when you travel or visit family during the holidays, then this is the perfect book for you.

Prepare to laugh, gasp, and shake your head in confusion as we enter a world of facts and knowledge.

Assorted Fun Facts to Warm Up

1. The stapes is the smallest bone in the human body, it is in the middle ear.

_____

2. The United States has the most tornadoes of any country. Canada is second.

_____

3. Like fingerprints, everybody has a unique tongue print.

_____

4. A cow's stomach has four different compartments to it.

_____

5. Portuguese is the official and national language of Brazil, after being the only country colonized by the Portuguese in the Americas.

_____

6. The United States, Canada, Russia, Greenland, and Norway are the five different countries each with a population of polar bears.

_____

7. The Earth and our Solar System are in the Milky Way galaxy.

_____

8. Orville and Wilbur Wright (The Wright Brothers) created the first successful airplane.

_____

9. Kangaroos can't walk backwards.

_____

10. Russia is the largest country in the world.

_____

11. Astronauts can grow up to 3 inches taller in space as there is less gravity.

_____

12. Earthworms have five pairs of hearts.

_____

13. The sun is a star.

_____

14. Hot water will turn to ice faster than cold water.

_____

15. Dr. John Pemberton invented Coca-Cola in 1886.

_____

16. 92.5% of an Olympic gold medal is made from silver.

_____

17. Dutch painter Vincent van Gogh only sold one painting while he was alive.

_____

18. Origami comes from two Japanese words: ori (folding) and kami (paper).

_____

19. An octopus has blue blood.

_____

20. The word spam comes from a combination of the words spice and ham.

_____

21. Abraham Lincoln was the 16th President of the United States and a former professional wrestler.

_____

22. The heart of a shrimp is in its head.

_____

23. The skull and crossbones flag at the top of a pirate ship is called a Jolly Roger.

_____

24. NASA stands for National Aeronautics and Space Administration.

---

25. Sofia is the capital city of Bulgaria.

---

26. Avocados are a fruit, not a vegetable.

---

27. Baby rabbits are called kittens or kits.

---

28. M&Ms are named after their creators Forrest Mars and Bruce Murrie.

---

29. Angel Falls in Venezuela is the tallest waterfall in the world.

---

30. The small dot over a lowercase "i" and "j" is called a "tittle".

---

31. On April 15, 1912, the RMS Titanic sunk in the North Atlantic Ocean.

---

32. Russia has eleven time zones.

---

33. Vatican City is the smallest country in the world.

---

34. Slugs have four noses.

---

35. A cul-de-sac has no through road or no exit road. It's a road with only one way in and one way out.

---

36. There are no mosquitoes in Iceland.

---

37. Bananas are curved because of negative geotropism. That means they grow against gravity, and instead, turn up towards the sun.

---

38. Saint Lucia was named after Saint Lucy of Syracuse (AD 283 − 304).

39. Jousting became the official sport of Maryland in 1962.

---

40. The Corn Islands are two islands located in the Caribbean Sea of Nicaragua.

---

41. Manga are comics or graphic novels originating from Japan.

_____

42. A baby puffin is called a puffling.

_____

43. Snowboarding first became an Olympic sport in 1998 in Nagano, Japan.

_____

44. A fear of bridges and tunnels is called gephyrophobia.

_____

45. The United Nations was created in 1945 in San Francisco, California, United States.

_____

46. The Starbucks logo is a two-tailed mermaid called "Siren".

_____

47. Asia is the largest continent on Earth by size.

_____

48. Sharks don't have bones, instead, they have cartilage.

_____

49. Hawaiian pizza was invented in Ontario, Canada by Sam Panopoulos.

_____

50. Good morning in Spanish is "Buenos días".

_____

51. AB negative is the rarest blood type.

---

52. In 1995 the potato became the first vegetable grown in space.

---

53. Santiago is the capital of Chile.

---

54. In Greek mythology, Nike is the goddess of victory.

---

55. Yoda from Star Wars got his appearance based on a poster of Albert Einstein.

---

56. The chemical symbol of water is H_2O.

---

57. ASAP is an abbreviation for "as soon as possible".

---

58. Dreamt is the only word in the English language that ends with "mt".

---

59. Opera singer Luciano Pavarotti was born in Modena, Italy in 1935.

---

60. J.K. Rowling found inspiration for the setting of "*Harry Potter*" in Edinburgh, Scotland.

---

61. Maine is the only state in the United States that has only one syllable in its name.

_____

62. Nelson Mandela was the president of South Africa from 1994 to 1999.

_____

63. The capital city of Ethiopia is Addis Ababa.

_____

64. Mosquitoes are common carriers of malaria.

_____

65. The Indian Rupee is the official currency of India.

_____

66. Butterflies have four wings, not two.

_____

67. The first Penguin paperback books were published in 1935.

_____

68. The ancient Egyptians used the stem of the papyrus plant to make paper.

69. The nation of Sudan has more pyramids than Egypt.

70. A big portion of household dust is made up of dead skin cells.

71. The Philippines consists of 7,641 islands.

72. "Spaghetto" is the singular word for spaghetti.

73. Roman numerals start from one and had no symbol to represent zero.

---

74. Buddha was born with the name Siddhartha Gautama.

---

75. Anteaters don't have any teeth.

---

76. The dwarf planet Pluto was named after the Roman god of the underworld.

---

77. On the periodic table of elements, Gold's symbol is Au.

---

78. Violin bows are usually made from horsehair.

---

79. A matador is a man who fights bulls.

---

80. Pugilism is a Latin word for the sport of boxing.

---

81. A small group of bananas is called a hand, and an entire stalk of bananas is called a bunch.

---

82. Pumas are carnivores, they hunt and eat other animals to survive.

---

83. Reggae is a music genre that originated in Jamaica in the late 1960s.

---

84. A favela is a shantytown or slum area found in Brazil.

---

85. Julius Caesar was kidnapped by pirates in 75 BC while journeying across the Aegean Sea.

---

86. Victorians used a device to predict the weather by getting leeches to ring a bell.

---

87. The funny bone isn't a bone, it's an ulnar nerve.

---

88. Arachnophobia is an intense fear of spiders.

---

89. Helen Keller was the first deaf and blind person to earn a college degree.

---

90. German is the official language of Austria.

---

91. Gazelles can shrink their heart and liver to survive in heat and drought.

---

92. The Incas used strings and knots to keep records; this was called "quipu" (khipu).

93. A "cabbie" is an informal British term for a taxicab driver.

92. Gazelles can shrink their heart and liver to survive in heat and drought.

93. The Incas used strings and knots to keep records; this was called "quipu" (khipu).

94. Water bottles have an expiry date because the plastic will eventually leak chemicals into the water, not because the water expires or goes bad.

95. A drone is a male honeybee; they don't have stingers.

96. The Battle of Hastings was fought on 14 October 1066 with the Norman-French army triumphing over the English army.

97. Brazil is the world's largest producer of coffee.

---

98. The Declaration of Independence of the United States from Great Britain was adopted on July 4, 1776.

---

99. Rubber comes from the sap of a tree called the Hevea brasiliensis tree which originated in South America.

---

100. Flamingos eat with their head upside down.

A Mixed Cauldron of Random Facts

101. The Sahara is the world's largest desert.

---

102. A group of owls is called a parliament.

---

103. Wolfgang Amadeus Mozart was born in Salzburg, Austria.

---

104. Usain Bolt won 8 Olympic gold medals.

---

105. Babies are born with 300 bones, whereas adults only have 206 bones.

---

106. Chickens eat a wide variety of local vegetation, grasses, herbs, seeds, berries, worms, insects, snails, and even slugs.

---

107. The United States is the biggest producer of cheese in the world.

---

108. Fortune Telling is illegal in Baltimore, Maryland.

---

109. The language spoken in Korea is called Hangul.

---

110. Leonardo Da Vinci painted the *"Mona Lisa"*. It's kept at the Louvre Museum in Paris, France.

---

111. Amman is the capital of Jordan.

---

112. Elephants can't jump.

---

113. Tug of war was featured at five Olympic Games between 1900 and 1920.

---

114. The word armadillo means "little armoured one" in Spanish.

---

115. The modern pizza was first invented in Naples, Italy.

---

116. An earthquake under the ocean can cause tsunamis.

---

117. Japan has an eel (Unagi Aisu) and crab (Kani Aisu) flavoured ice cream.

---

118. Bobcats are the smallest cats in the lynx species.

119. Alexander the Great became king of the ancient Greek kingdom of Macedonia after succeeding his father King Phillip II at just 20 years of age.

---

120. The Mugunghwa, or Rose of Sharon (Hibiscus syriacus), is the national flower of South Korea.

---

121. Orcas have evolved to swim up to 40 miles a day, searching for food provisions and exercising.

---

122. The unicorn is the national animal of Scotland.

---

123. A republic is a government without a king or queen.

---

124. There are no bridges across the Amazon River.

---

125. Crocodiles cannot stick their tongues out.

---

126. "..." is called an ellipsis.

---

127. A rabbit's teeth have open roots and never stop growing.

---

128. Nemo from the movie *"Finding Nemo"* is a clownfish and Dory is a regal blue tang fish.

---

129. The car manufacturer Volkswagen produces more sausages than cars.

---

130. Diamonds are the hardest naturally occurring substance on Earth.

---

131 Bats give birth hanging upside down.

---

132. Like earthquakes, the moon has moonquakes.

_____

133. "Blackbeard", the nickname of Edward Teach, is one of history's most famous pirates.

_____

134. The first floppy disk was introduced in 1971.

_____

135. Sugar cane is mainly used to make sugar.

136. The Siamese cat is native to Thailand.

_____

137. Giraffes are the tallest mammals on Earth.

---

138. The letter "E" is the most used letter in the alphabet.

---

139. Lacrosse is the national summer sport of Canada.

---

140. The Statue of Liberty was gifted by France to the United States in 1885 to celebrate their friendship.

---

141. The blob of toothpaste sitting on your toothbrush is called a "nurdle".

---

142. Bullet ants are thought to have the most painful sting in the world.

---

143. The River Severn is United Kingdom's longest river.

---

144. Samsung means "three stars" in Korean.

---

145. The Scott Paper Company was the first bathroom tissue maker to insert a cardboard tube into the roll, back in 1890.

---

146. Summer on Uranus lasts for 21 years.

---

147. The first version of Monopoly was invented back in 1902 by Elizabeth Magie, it was called *"The Landlord's Game"*.

---

148. Alexander Fleming discovered penicillin.

---

149. The Vikings referred to themselves as Ostmen and were also known as Norsemen, Norse and Danes.

---

150. A human liver can regenerate by replacing damaged tissue.

---

151. In France, French toast is called pain perdu which means "lost bread".

---

152. The Loch Ness Monster, or Nessie, is a creature in Scottish Folklore that allegedly lives in Loch Ness Lake near Inverness, Scotland.

---

153. Accra is the capital city of the West African nation of Ghana.

---

154. Football (also known as soccer or fútbol) is the most popular sport in the world.

---

155. Jazz music originated in New Orleans, Louisiana, United States.

156. The main ingredient in plastic comes from chemicals found in fossil fuels such as natural gas and crude oil.

157. BTS are the highest-earning K-pop group in South Korea.

158. Cacerolazo, Spanish for casserole, is a way to protest involving pot-banging famous in Latin America.

159. Baseball is the most popular sport in the Dominican Republic.

160. Mushrooms are fungi, they are separate from plants and animals.

161. Clouds appear white because the light from the sun is white.

162. Bats are nocturnal, they only come out at night.

163. The first candy canes in history had no stripes.

164. New Zealand has more sheep than people.

___

165. The estimated percentage of left-handed people worldwide is only 10-12%.

___

166. Mercury is the smallest planet in our solar system.

___

167. There are 27 stars on the Brazilian flag.

___

168. The lead of a pencil is made up of graphite and clay powders.

___

169. An invertebrate is an animal with no backbone.

___

170. A cube has 12 edges.

___

171. Flamingo chicks hatch with white-grey feathers, not pink.

___

CAPE TOWN

172. Cape Town, South Africa is also known as the "Mother City".

---

173. The chemical symbol for iron is Fe.

---

174. Each polo team is made up of four players.

---

175. To run for President of the United States the candidate must be 35 years of age.

---

176. A group of giraffes is called a tower.

---

177. Julie Andrews played Mary Poppins in the 1964 film Mary Poppins.

---

178. Claude Monet painted *"The Water Lily Pond"* in 1899.

---

179. Stonehenge is a prehistoric monument that stands in Wiltshire, England.

___

180. Human blood contains salt that is very similar to seawater.

___

181. The Danish krone is the official currency of Denmark.

___

182. The Black Death or bubonic plague was the deadliest pandemic in history.

___

183. In Norse mythology, the gods lived in Asgard.

___

184. Mount Everest is the tallest mountain in the world.

___

185. Most dogs have 42 adult canine teeth.

___

186. A nautical mile is 1.15 miles.

___

187. In the 19th century, Victorian photographers said "prunes" instead of "cheese" to smile for the camera.

___

188. A heptadecagon has 17 sides.

___

189. The surname Singh originates from the Sanskrit word meaning "lion".

---

190. A polygraph is popularly known as a lie detector test.

---

191. Spanish artist, Salvador Dali sculpted the *"Lobster Telephone"* in 1936.

---

192. Brussels, Belgium, is the headquarters of the European Union.

---

193. Sacramento is the capital of the U.S state of California.

---

194. The tulip is the national flower of the Netherlands.

---

195. James Matthew Barrie wrote *"Peter Pan"*.

---

196. DVD stands for "Digital Versatile Disc".

---

197. Baku is the capital city of Azerbaijan.

---

198. Barack Obama served as the 44th President of the United States.

---

199. On a calculator, "AC" means All Clear.

_____

200. Chalk is made up of fossils.

_____

201. In Ancient Rome, a female gladiator was called a Gladiatrix.

---

202. Batman first appeared in Detective Comics #27 in May 1939.

---

203. In Greek mythology, Medusa had a head of hair consisting of snakes.

---

204. Ancient Rome had take-out restaurants called thermopolia.

---

205. In ancient Greece the unibrow was considered a symbol of beauty for women. Some women would even paint the gap between their eyebrows to give the appearance of one eyebrow.

---

206. The University of Oxford was founded in 1096.

---

207. John Adams was the first president to live in the White House.

208. Abraham Lincoln was a championship wrestler.

---

209. A sphinx has a body of a lion and the head of a human.

---

210. People were accused of being witches during the Salem witch trials from 1692 and 1693.

---

211. Julius Caesar was the first Roman to invade Great Britain.

---

212. Ancient Egyptians used stone slabs to support the heads of dead people.

_____

213. Israel asked Albert Einstein to be their president.

_____

214. Klerksdorp spheres were dug up in South Africa and are billions of years old.

_____

215. A Roman soldier's helmet was called a "galea".

_____

216. Some Japanese women fought alongside Samurai warriors.

_____

217. Queen Elizabeth I enjoyed eating sugar and sweets.

_____

218. The Tyrannosaurus rex or T. rex became extinct 65 million years ago.

_____

219. Before the 1950s boys were dressed in pink and girls in blue.

_____

220. José Rizal is considered a national hero of the Philippines for fighting peacefully against the Spanish.

_____

221. British tanks have tea making equipment.

___

222. Pythagoras didn't eat fava beans.

___

223. Cuba has more 1950s cars in operation than any other country.

___

224. Mr. Potato Head was the first toy to be advertised on television.

___

225. Chinese women used to bind their feet.

___

226. Joan of Arc was the inspiration behind the bob haircut.

___

227. William Henry Harrison was U.S. president for only one month before he died.

___

228. Iceland's parliament, Althing, was founded in 930.

___

229. The Eiffel Tower is named after the French engineer Gustave Eiffel.

___

230. Nintendo originally made playing cards.

___

231. The first McDonald's was opened in San Bernadino, California.

---

232. Construction started on the Brooklyn Bridge in 1869 and the bridge opened in 1883.

---

233. Over the past few centuries, people's average height has gotten taller.

---

234. In Roman times, Scotland was called Caledonia.

235. The Great Fire of London started in a baker's house in Pudding Lane.

---

236. Quarantine began in 14th century Venice due to the 40-day isolation of ships to prevent the plague.

---

237. Track and field athlete Jessie Owens won four gold medals at the 1936 Berlin Olympics.

---

238. Indonesia used to be known as the Dutch East Indies.

---

239. In Britain and Ireland, before alarm clocks, a "knocker-up" would wake up sleeping people for work.

---

240. Howard Carter discovered Tutankhamun's tomb.

---

241. Dinosaurs lived on all continents.

---

242. Anyone who looked into Medusa's eyes would turn to stone.

---

243. The CIA tried to train cats to be a spy.

---

244. Istanbul in Turkey used to be called Constantinople.

---

245. Elvis Presley received a "C" grade for music in the eighth grade.

---

246. Tempus is a Latin word meaning time.

---

247. England has only won the men's Football FIFA World Cup one time, in 1966.

---

248. The five rings on the Olympic flag represent the five continents.

---

249. Some Viking men dyed their hair blonde.

---

250. Victorian people took photographs after their loved ones had died to remember them.

Famous Inventions and Discoveries to Inspire Young Creators

251. The metal aluminium was first isolated by Hans Christian Ørsted in 1825 in Copenhagen, Denmark.

---

252. Kellogg's cornflakes were originally made with wheat.

---

253. The electric car company Tesla is named after the inventor Nikola Tesla.

---

254. Percy Shaw came up with the idea for cat eyes to light up a road's surface one night during a foggy drive.

---

255. Amazon was founded in Jeff Bezos' garage in Bellevue, Washington back in 1994.

---

256. Popsicles were originally called "epsicles" after the inventor Frank Epperson.

---

257. Petra, Jordan is called the "Lost City" because it wasn't discovered until 1812.

---

258. Joseph Armand Bombardier started working on the snowmobile when he was just 19 years old.

259. Tetris was first made in Moscow, Russia.

260. Sony was founded in Tokyo, Japan.

261. The original Starbucks Coffee shop is at 1912 Pike Place in Seattle, Washington.

262. Alfred Nobel invented dynamite in 1867.

263. The Otis Elevator Company is named after the founder of the elevator, Elisha Otis.

264. Google's headquarters is in Mountain View, California, United States.

265. The world's first steam train to carry passengers was called Locomotion No. 1.

266. In 1637, the first public opera house called the Teatro San Cassiano opened in Venice, Italy.

267. WWW is an acronym for "World Wide Web".

268. Rudolph "Rudi" Dassler is the founder of Puma, his older brother Adolph "Adi" Dassler started Adidas.

269. The BBC or British Broadcasting Corporation is the national broadcasting station of the United Kingdom.

270. The first smartphone was invented in 1992 by IBM and was named the Simon.

271. The famous rock band "The Beatles" were formed in Liverpool, England.

272. E-mail stands for "electronic mail".

273. Galileo Galilei discovered the four moons of Jupiter.

---

274. Paper was first used in Ancient China.

---

275. Cathay Pacific Airlines operates out of Hong Kong.

---

276. *"The Lion, the Witch, and the Wardrobe"* fantasy novel for children was written by C.S. Lewis.

---

277. Car manufacturer BMW was founded in Munich, Germany.

---

278. The saxophone was invented by Adolphe Sax.

---

279. The Empire State Building in New York took 1 year and 45 days to build.

---

280. Chess was invented in India.

---

281. Traffic lights are known as "robots" in South Africa.

---

282. The asteroid 16 Psyche is thought to contain gold.

---

283. Mars Bars were first produced in 1932.

---

284. The Romans built aqueducts to transport water.

---

285. CD stands for "compact disc".

286. The Chinese Terracotta Army sculptures were discovered in 1974 by some farmers.

---

287. Canberra was named the capital of Australia in 1913.

---

288. The inventor of bubblegum, Walter Diemer admitted he discovered it "by accident".

---

289. Benjamin Franklin invented the lightning rod.

---

290. Morse Code is named after Samuel Morse.

---

291. The first lava lamp was launched in 1963.

---

292. An LP record stands for a "Long Play" record.

---

293. The first glass of Coca-Cola was sold at Jacobs' Pharmacy in downtown Atlanta.

---

294. Johann Christoph Denner invented the clarinet in Nuremberg, Germany.

---

295. Microscopes make small objects appear larger.

---

296. Hieroglyphs were a picture writing system used in ancient Egypt.

---

297. A compass is used to find direction.

---

298. Satellite Navigation or GPS stands for "Global Positioning System".

---

299. The first microwave was known as the "Radarange".

---

300. A packet of Wrigley's Chewing Gum was the first-ever barcode to have a barcode.

Geography and Landmarks for Potential World Explorers

301. Some of the *"Tomb Raider"* movie was filmed at Angkor Wat in Cambodia.

302. The Leaning Tower of Pisa has always been tilted.

303. Damascus, Syria is known as the "City of Jasmine".

304. Bali is an island in Indonesia.

305. The Netherlands is also known as Holland.

306. The Taj Mahal in Agra, India is made of ivory-white marble.

307. Lima is the capital city of Peru.

308. The Canary Islands belong to Spain.

309. Wadi Rum in Jordan is also known as the "Valley of the Moon" because it looks like the surface of the moon.

310. The Great Sphinx sits guard over the Pyramids of Giza in Cairo, Egypt.

311. The longest river in Africa is the Nile River.

312. Chicago, United States is also nicknamed the "Windy City".

313. Iran used to be called Persia.

314. The Port of Rotterdam in the Netherlands is the biggest port in Europe.

---

315. Mount Kilimanjaro is in Tanzania.

---

316. The Amazon is the largest rainforest in the world.

---

317. Niagara Falls is made up of three waterfalls.

---

318. Taipei 101 is the tallest building in Taiwan.

---

319. The Ruble is the currency of Russia.

---

320. Harvard University is in the state of Massachusetts, United States.

---

321. Montevideo is the capital city of Uruguay.

---

322. There is a Little Mermaid statue in Copenhagen, Denmark.

---

323. The official languages of Belgium are Dutch, French, and German.

---

324. Rome, Italy is also known as the "Eternal City".

---

325. The Ganges is a holy river in India.

---

326. Santorini in Greece has lots of churches with blue domes.

---

327. The flag of Ireland is a vertical tricolour of green, white, and orange.

---

328. Sri Lanka used to be called Ceylon.

---

329. The Great Wall of China is one of the seven Wonders of the World.

---

330. Fiji is an island in the Pacific Ocean.

---

331. The government building in Moscow, Russia is called the Kremlin.

---

332. There is a building in London nicknamed "The Gherkin" because it looks like a small cucumber.

---

333. The Everglades national park in Florida, United States is famous for having alligators.

---

334. Tundra is a treeless area where the soil is permanently frozen.

---

335. There is a golden sun in the middle of the flag of Argentina.

---

336. Asia is the largest continent in size.

---

337. The duck-billed platypus is an animal native to Australia.

---

338. The Golden Gate Bridge is in San Francisco, United States.

---

339. Riyadh is the capital city of Saudi Arabia.

---

340. There are over 1000 windmills in the Netherlands.

---

341. Nigeria has the largest population of all the African nations.

---

342. The official language of Hungary is Hungarian.

---

343. *"Marcha Real"* is the national anthem of Spain, it has no words.

344. The Angel of the North statue is in Gateshead, England.

345. There is a maple leaf on the Canadian flag.

346. The Japanese yen is the currency of Japan.

347. Freshwater is available in Antarctica frozen in ice.

348. Table Mountain overlooks the city of Cape Town, South Africa.

349. The Great Mosque of Djenné is in Mali.

350. Madagascar is in the Indian Ocean.

351. The largest pyramid in the world is in Cholula, Mexico.

___

352. Edinburgh, Glasgow, and Dundee are all cities in Scotland.

___

353. Tourists kiss the Blarney Stone in Cork, Ireland.

___

354. Mexico is in North America.

___

355. In its early days, Melbourne, Australia was known as Bearbrass.

___

356. Lake Victoria is the largest lake in Africa.

___

357. Gondolas are used on the canals of Venice, Italy.

___

358. Mount Fuji is the highest point in Japan.

___

359. In Chinese, Hong Kong means "Fragrant Harbour".

___

360. A dune is a hill made of sand.

___

361. Kangaroo Island is in Australia.

___

362. The Northern Lights are also known as "aurora borealis".

363. Brazil is the largest country in South America.

364. The deepest part of the ocean is called the Mariana Trench in the Pacific Ocean.

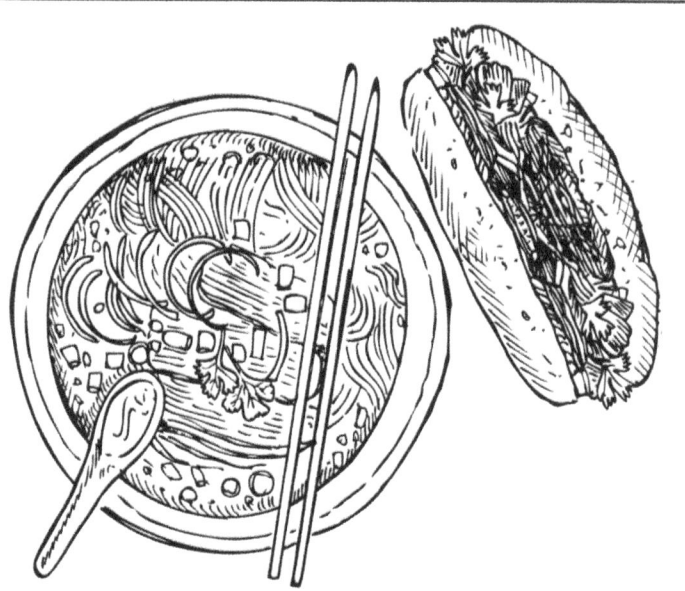

365. Pho and bánh mì are famous Vietnamese foods.

366. The Grand Canyon is in Arizona, United States.

367. Kuala Lumpur is the capital city of Malaysia.

368. Varanasi is the religious capital of India.

---

369. There is only one time-zone in China.

---

370. In Chile, people speak Spanish.

---

371. Mozambique is the only country with a single-word name that uses all five vowels.

---

372. China is the most populated country in the world.

---

373. The international airport of Liverpool England is named Liverpool John Lennon Airport.

---

374. The Great Barrier Reef in Australia is the world's largest coral reef.

---

375. O'Hare International Airport is in Chicago, United States.

---

376. A river delta is triangle shaped.

---

377. Iceland is also known as "the land of fire and ice".

---

378. The two Bactrian or two-humped camel is native to Mongolia.

---

379. Manilla is the capital of the Philippines.

---

380. The Hanging Gardens of Babylon are in Iraq.

---

381. Lithuania is in Europe.

---

382. Australia is the smallest continent.

---

383. It has snowed in the Sahara Desert before.

---

384. Sicily is the largest island in the Mediterranean Sea.

---

385. The Suez Canal in Egypt connects trade between Europe and Asia.

---

386. There are more than 1000 fjords in Norway.

---

387. Myanmar used to be known as Burma.

---

388. Tangier is a coastal town in Morocco.

---

389. Dodo birds used to live on the island of Mauritius before they became extinct.

---

390. Christopher Columbus gave Honduras its name which means "depths" in Spanish.

---

391. New Delhi is the capital of India.

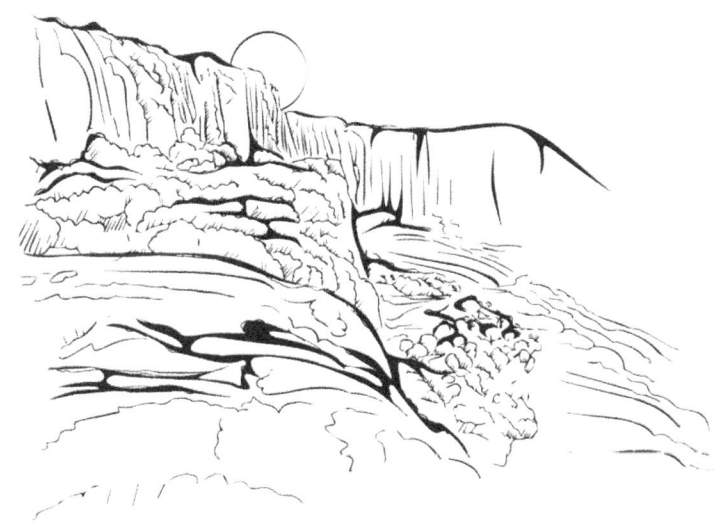

392. Victoria Falls forms a border between Zambia and Zimbabwe.

---

393. The South Pole is much colder than the North Pole.

---

394. The Maya people built Chichen Itza in Mexico.

_____

395. A series of mountains is called a range.

_____

396. The Tigris River runs through Baghdad, Iraq.

_____

397. Marseille is in France.

_____

398. Lake Superior is the largest lake in North America.

_____

399. The Andes are a mountain range in South America.

_____

400. South Africa has three capital cities: Cape Town, Pretoria, and Bloemfontein.

_____

401. Tasmania is the largest island state in Australia.

_____

402. The River Clyde flows through Glasgow, Scotland.

_____

403. The Port of Shanghai in China is the biggest port in the world.

_____

404. Zimbabwe used to be called Rhodesia.

_____

405. Brazil has land borders with ten countries.

___

406. The Turkish lira is the official currency of Turkey.

___

407. Jakarta is the capital city of Indonesia.

___

408. Antwerp, Belgium is famous for its diamond industry.

___

409. Goulash is a national dish of Hungary.

___

410. Amsterdam is the largest city in the Netherlands.

___

411. The Equator is located halfway between the North Pole and the South Pole.

___

412. Qatar is the only country in the world beginning with the letter "Q".

___

413. Tacos are a traditional Mexican dish.

___

414. Barbados is an island in the Caribbean.

___

415. More than half of Sweden is covered in forests.

___

416. The Japanese flag has a red circle on a white background.

---

417. Toledo, Ohio, United States is famous for glass manufacturing.

---

418. The world's biggest swimming pool is in Algarrobo, Chile.

419. Windsor Castle is one of the residences of Queen Elizabeth II.

---

420. Meteorology is the study of the weather.

___

421. The Cook Islands were named after the British explorer James Cook.

___

422. Denmark used to rule Iceland.

___

423. Nuuk is the capital city of Greenland.

___

424. Tropical climates are closer to the Equator where there is more direct sunlight.

___

425. The CN Tower is in Toronto, Canada.

___

426. Mother Teresa was born in Skopje, North Macedonia.

___

427. Tteokbokki is a spicy rice cake from Korea.

___

428. To toast or say cheers in German, people say "prost".

___

429. Cuba is the largest Caribbean Island.

___

430. A coniferous tree grows pinecones.

___

431. Costa Rica is one of the world's biggest pineapple producers.

432. A drought is a shortage of water supplies caused by a long period without rain.

433. A map helps you to locate a place.

434. The flag of Wales has a red dragon on it.

435. Oukaïmeden in Morocco is Africa's biggest ski resort.

436. The North Sea separates the United Kingdom and Denmark.

437. Quarries are where rocks are extracted from the ground.

438. The city of Aden is in Yemen.

439. Portugal shares a border with Spain.

440. Vienna is the capital city of Austria.

441. Before the Euro, Germany's currency was the Deutsche Mark.

---

442. The Maracanã Stadium in Rio de Janeiro is the biggest football stadium in Brazil.

---

443. The Batu Caves are a famous Hindu sight in Malaysia.

444. San Marino is a landlocked country surrounded by Italy.

---

445. There are four countries in the United Kingdom: England, Wales, Scotland, and Northern Ireland.

---

446. Whistler Ski Resort is in British Columbia, Canada.

---

447. The Galápagos Islands have active volcanoes.

---

448. Nepal is a country in Asia.

---

449. Dubai and Abu Dhabi are in the United Arab Emirates.

---

450. The Kelpies are huge horse head sculptures in Falkirk, Scotland. They represent the horse-like creature that can shapeshift into a human in Scottish folklore.

Funny and Weird Facts for Your Friends

451. In Space, no one can hear you fart (but they can smell it).

---

452. You can bid for a piece of meteorite on eBay.

---

453. If you spell racecar backwards it spells racecar.

---

454. Saudi Arabia has no permanent rivers.

---

455. There are no poisonous snakes in Alaska, United States.

---

456. China produces the most eggs in the world.

---

457. The bird on the Twitter logo is called Larry T. Bird after the basketballer Larry Bird.

---

458. Dust from the Sahara Desert can travel all the way to the Amazon Rainforest.

---

459. The small intestine is longer than the large intestine.

---

460. Uranus used to be called "the Georgium Sidus" which means the Georgian Planet, it was named after King George III.

461. Ninety Mile Beach in New Zealand is only actually 55 miles long.

462. Panama Hats are made in Ecuador, not Panama.

463. A group of pandas is called an embarrassment.

464. Kiwifruit originated in China, not New Zealand.

465. Octopuses have three hearts.

466. Canadians eat the most Kraft Macaroni and Cheese of any country in the world.

467. Hedgehogs often yawn.

468. A set of Lego Minifigures was launched into space on the 2011 NASA Juno mission to Jupiter.

469. There is an island in the Bahamas called Pig Beach.

470. Some tonsils can grow back if after being removed if there is some tissue left.

_____

471. Kangaroos never stop growing until they die.

_____

472. Lachanophobia is the name for someone who fears vegetables.

_____

473. American golf balls usually have 366 dimples on them by regulation.

_____

474. There are wigs for dogs in Tokyo, Japan.

_____

475. Recycling glass saves energy.

_____

476. Casu marzu is cheese from Sardinia that contains live maggots.

_____

477. Alan Shepard of Apollo 14 played golf on the moon.

_____

478. Queen Elizabeth II has a fondness for Pembroke Welsh corgis.

_____

479. There is a town called Santa Claus in Indiana, United States.

_____

480. Potato skins have more nutrients than the interior of the potato.

_____

481. Association football or soccer was created in England in 1863.

_____

482. San Francisco's cable cars are considered National Monuments.

_____

483. There are no roads in the town of Giethoorn, Netherlands.

_____

484. The Amazon River is home to the pink river dolphin or boto.

_____

485. Moonbows are rainbows produced by moonlight instead of direct light from the sun.

_____

486. Fresh cranberries can bounce.

_____

487. The femur, or thigh bone, is the biggest bone in the human body.

_____

488. Using headphones dramatically increases bacteria in the ear.

---

489. Male mosquitoes can't bite, only female mosquitoes can.

---

490. There are no words in the English language that rhyme with "orange" and "purple".

---

491. In Ancient Greece and Rome, doctors would use spider webs as bandages for their patients.

---

492. Densuke watermelons from Japan are the most expensive watermelons in the world.

---

493. The Haskell Free Library and Opera House is located across the United States and Canadian border.

---

494. Gray foxes can retract their claws.

---

495. Eyelid skin is the thinnest skin on the human body.

---

496. The kākāpō bird is the world's only flightless parrot.

---

497. Tigers have striped skin as well as striped fur.

---

498. Porcupines can float in water.

_____

499. The word "screeched" is only one syllable.

_____

500. Lake Retba is a pink lake in Senegal.

_____

A Quick Pause...

If this book has helped you in any way, we'd appreciate it if you left us a review on Amazon. Reviews are the lifeblood of our business. We read every single one and incorporate your feedback into our future book projects.

To leave an Amazon review please visit https://www.amazon.com/ryp or scan the QR code below...THANK YOU!

Pick and Mix Facts

501. Oil is a non-renewable source, it cannot be replaced.

502. Saint Patrick is the patron saint of Ireland.

503. Wimbledon is the oldest tennis tournament in the world, it began on 9 July 1877.

504. The game *"Angry Birds"* was created in Finland by Rovio Entertainment.

505. The heart has four valves.

506. Brasília became Brazil's capital in 1960.

507. The sun is mostly made up of hydrogen gas.

_____

508. Ricotta cheese originated in Italy.

_____

509. The chemical symbol for tin is Sn.

_____

510. Easter always falls on a Sunday.

_____

511. Astronomy is the study of the universe and natural objects in space.

_____

512. Chocolate is made from cocoa beans.

_____

513. Mario from *"Super Mario"* is an Italian plumber.

_____

514. Cats can hear ultrasound with a frequency greater than the limit of human hearing.

_____

515. A pumpkin carved at Halloween is called a Jack -o'- Lantern.

_____

516. Albania is in Europe.

_____

517. A baby goose is called a gosling.

---

518. There are 21 dots on one dice and 42 dots on a pair of dice.

---

519. A grouping of twelve is often referred to as a dozen.

---

520. An epitaph is the writing on a tomb or grave.

---

521. The Lincoln Memorial is in Washington D.C., United States.

---

522. There are 25.4mm in an inch.

---

523. The Orange River is the largest river in South Africa.

---

524. Citrus fruits are rich in Vitamin C.

---

525. The Basenji dog cannot bark.

---

526. Crab spiders have eight eyes.

---

527. Santa Claus is known as Sinterklaas in Dutch.

528. The Statue of Liberty wears a crown with seven spikes.

529. Google was originally named BackRub.

530. The board game of checkers is much older than chess.

531. Africa's ostrich is the fastest running bird in the world.

532. USB stands for "universal serial bus".

533. The 13 stripes on the United States flag represent the original colonies.

534. The name Pinocchio combines the Italian words "pino" (pine) and "occhio" (eye).

535. Caesar Augustus was the first Roman emperor.

536. Butterflies have four wings.

537. Walt Disney World Resort in Orlando, Florida is the biggest theme park in the world.

538. The Lady Lever Art Gallery is in Liverpool, England.

539. Birds migrate to suit their food and nesting needs.

540. The car manufacturer Škoda was founded in the Czech Republic.

541. A gathering of witches is called a coven.

542. Elon Musk founded SpaceX in 2002.

543. Texas is officially nicknamed "The Lone Star State".

544. Montego Bay is in Jamaica.

---

545. Smoke added to fog creates smog in the atmosphere.

---

546. An elephant has four knees.

---

547. "Feliz Navidad" is Merry Christmas in Spanish.

---

548. Botany is the study of science relating to plants.

---

549. The highest score possible in ten-pin bowling is 300.

---

550. Snow White is the first and oldest Disney princess, she first appeared in 1937.

---

551. The first Tour de France cycling race was held in 1903 and was won by Maurice Garin of France.

---

552. Ireland is known as "The Emerald Isle" due to its green landscape.

---

553. In the Bible, the wise men brought to Jesus: gold, frankincense (an incense), and myrrh (an embalming oil).

---

554. The Snellen Chart is used to test the eyes.

555. Yuri Gagarin was the first human to fly to space in 1961.

556. In badminton, players hit a shuttlecock over the next using their rackets.

557. Acrophobia is a fear of heights.

558. Cloud Gate is a bean sculpture by Anish Kapoor in Chicago, United States.

559. If something is submerged, it is underwater.

560. The Han River runs through the city of Seoul, South Korea.

561. The finger bones and toe bones are called "phalanges".

562. Tripoli is the capital city of Libya.

563. The Earth's atmosphere is made up of 21% Oxygen.

564. Charles de Gaulle airport is in Paris, France.

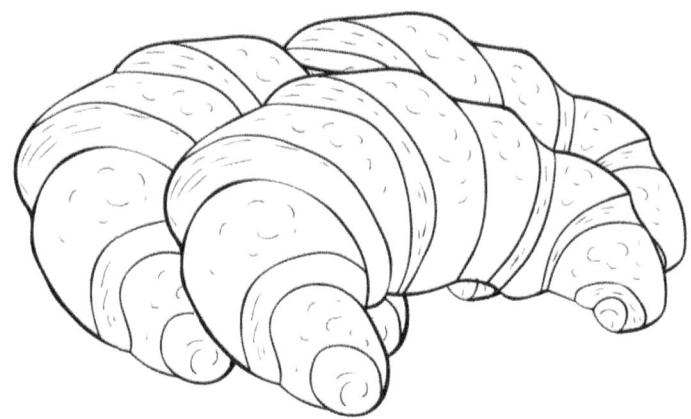

565. The kipferl is an early version of the croissant which can be traced back to 13th century Austria.

---

566. Kazakhstan is the largest landlocked country by area in the world.

---

567. The Richter Scale measures the magnitude of an earthquake.

---

568. According to Greek mythology, Pandora was the first woman on Earth.

---

569. Aardvarks can eat around 35,000 to 50,000 ants or termites every day.

---

570. Deciduous trees lose their leaves in winter.

---

571. Cheetahs are native to Africa and Asia.

_____

572. Dinosaurs first lived on Earth during the Triassic Period.

_____

573. Insects have six legs.

_____

574. The first wheelbarrows were invented in ancient China.

_____

575. Good Friday comes before Easter Sunday.

_____

576. Red diamonds are the rarest diamonds in the world.

_____

577. The Great Dane is the tallest breed of dog in the world.

_____

578. Indonesia is home to the Komodo dragon.

_____

579. The piece at the end of a shoelace is called an "aglet".

_____

580. Margaret Thatcher was the first female Prime Minister of the United Kingdom.

_____

581. The black mamba is the fastest land snake in the world reaching speeds of 10-12 mph.

_____

582. Humans have 12 pairs of ribs.

---

583. Brown is the most common eye colour in the world.

---

584. Private is the lowest rank of soldier in the United States Army.

---

585. Crocodiles can't stick their tongues out.

---

586. Confetto is the singular of confetti.

---

587. The Singapore Night Safari was the first one to open only at nighttime.

---

588. "*Gadsby*" is a 1939 novel written by Ernest Vincent Wright that doesn't contain the letter 'E' once.

---

589. Popping bubble wrap can be used as a stress reliever.

---

590. The 1st Extreme Ironing World Championships took place in 2002 with twelve teams competing for the title.

---

591. A period of 1000 years as calculated from the birth of Christ is known as a millennium.

---

592. Only four European countries still drive on the left side of the road: the United Kingdom, Ireland, Cyprus, and Malta.

---

593. Dermatology is the area of medicine that deals with the skin.

---

594. The first phone book was published in 1978 by the New Haven District Telephone Company in Connecticut, United States.

---

595. Dried plums are called prunes.

---

596. There is a museum of toilets in New Dehli, India called Sulabh International Museum of Toilets.

---

597. The dingo is a wild dog in Australia.

598. The United States president uses the airplane Air Force One to fly.

---

599. In Roman times, London was known as Londoninium and was the capital of Roman Britain.

---

600. An oak tree can be grown from an acorn.

Proof that Animals are Fascinating

601. A group of crows is called a murder.

_____

602. Domestic house cats and tigers share 95.6% of their DNA.

_____

603. A young bear is called a cub.

_____

604. Dalmatian puppies have no spots at birth.

_____

605. Starfish don't have a brain.

_____

606. Samoyed dogs get their name from the Samoyedic people of Siberia, Russia.

_____

607. Bats have thumbs.

_____

608. The neck of a giraffe is made up of seven bones.

_____

609. Mice teeth never stop growing throughout their lives.

_____

610. The megalodon, now extinct, is the largest shark that ever lived.

_____

611. Ostriches can run faster than horses.

_____

612. Lionesses hunt more than male lions.

_____

613. China has the largest population of pigs in the world.

_____

614. Young rhinos are called calves.

_____

615. Walruses can sleep in water and on land.

_____

616. Reindeer antlers fall off and grow back each year.

_____

617. The scientific term for the red fox is Vulpes vulpes.

_____

618. Scorpions glow blue-green under ultraviolet light.

_____

619. Koalas eat eucalyptus leaves.

_____

620. Badgers are very good at digging.

_____

621. Skunk odor can last up to three weeks.

_____

622. Bullsnakes are one of the largest snakes in North America.

_____

623. The emperor penguin is the largest penguin in the world.

_____

624. Newts can regenerate their limbs throughout their lives.

_____

625. Sockeye salmon change from blue to red.

_____

626. Woodpeckers have furry noses to keep splinters out while they peck.

---

627. Polar bears have the strongest bite of all bears.

---

628. Platypuses close their eyes underwater.

---

629. Wombats have cube-shaped poop.

---

630. Sea otters hold hands while they sleep to prevent themselves from drifting away.

---

631. Sea urchins live on the seabed of all five oceans.

---

632. The alpine ibex is a wild goat.

---

633. Giraffes can lick their own ears.

---

634. Pandas like to be alone.

---

635. Hummingbirds are the only birds that can fly backwards.

---

636. Adult mayflies only live for about 24 hours.

---

637. Turritopsis dohrnii is a jellyfish that can live forever.

_____

638. All lemurs are native to Madagascar.

_____

639. Tigers have rough tongues.

_____

640. Geckos have microscopic hairs called setae on their fingers which allow them to stick to any surface.

_____

641. Sloths digest food slower than any other mammal.

_____

642. The Florida panther was elected as Florida's state animal in 1982.

_____

643. The American bison is the largest land animal in North America.

_____

644. Dogs have sweat glands in their paws.

_____

645. Zoophobia is the fear of animals.

_____

646. Blue Jays are smart, they can even imitate the sound of hawks to warn other jays of danger.

_____

647. Pangolins can curl up into an armour-plated ball to prevent lions from eating it.

---

648. Whales have slow heartbeats.

---

649. Anglerfish have sharp and pointed fangs for catching prey.

---

650. Puffins are nicknamed sea parrots.

---

651. Elephants have unevenly scattered hair.

652. Oysters can change their gender back and forth.

---

653. Taurophobia is a fear of bulls.

---

654. A group of goats is a herd.

---

655. Wood frogs live all over North America.

---

656. Dolphins don't chew their food.

---

657. Xerus is another name for the African ground squirrel.

---

658. Emus are the second largest bird on Earth.

---

659. Bees have five eyes.

---

660. Ghost crabs are named so because they can camouflage into the sandy beaches.

---

661. Ferrets are related to polecats.

---

662. The horse fly has a painful bite.

---

663. The blue-eyed black lemur population is shrinking fast.

---

664. Butterflies can taste with their feet.

---

665. Reindeer eyeballs change colour from golden in the summer to blue in the winter.

---

666. Swans are covered in feathers.

---

667. Egyptian mau have spotted coats.

---

668. Cranes are a symbol of good fortune in Japan.

---

669. Frogs can jump high because of their springy legs.

---

670. Koalas have similar fingerprints to humans.

---

671. I hasapoo is a mix of Lhasa Apso and poodle dogs.

---

672. Colossus Penguins once existed.

---

673. A female deer is called a doe.

---

674. Male doves make a "cooing" sound.

---

675. Pandas like to eat bamboo.

676. The three-toed sloth is the slowest mammal in the world.

677. Lobsters have ten legs.

678. The kiwi bird is a national icon of New Zealand.

679. Cats were respected highly in Ancient Egypt.

680. Parrots can mimic human speech.

681. A ewe is a female sheep.

682. Cockroach hearts have 13 chambers.

---

683. Owls can rotate their heads in either direction at 270 degrees.

---

684. Pearls come from oysters.

---

685. The bald eagle is the national emblem of the United States.

---

686. A baby goat is called a kid.

---

687. The bearded vulture mostly eats bones.

---

688. Mandrills are the largest monkeys.

---

689. A rabbit's tail is called a "scut".

---

690. Groundhogs are also called "woodchucks".

---

691. "Dumbledore" is an old English word for bumblebee.

---

692. King cobras make nests.

---

693. Leafcutter ants can saw off leaves with their jaws.

694. Swai fish is a type of shark catfish native to Vietnam.

695. Highland cattle are a Scottish breed of cow.

696. Owls have small brains.

697. Fruit flies don't eat fruit.

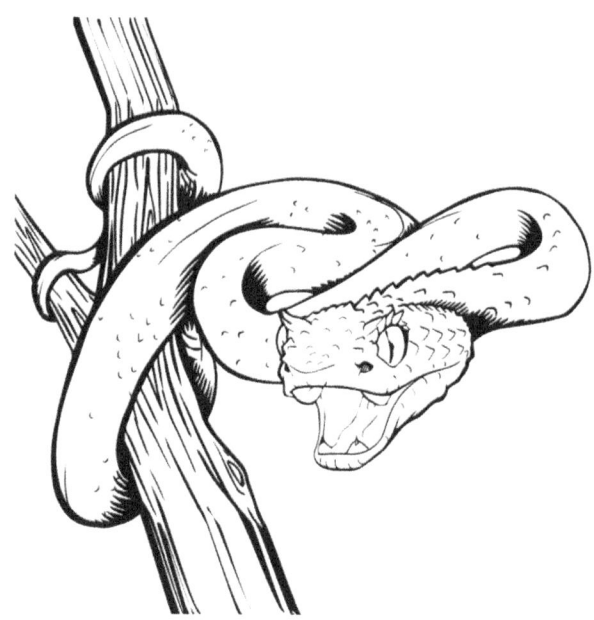

698. Eyelash vipers eat frogs.

699. Lungfish have both lungs and gills.

---

700. Alpacas are part of the camel family.

Facts to Help Launch Future Astronauts into Space

701. Nobody knows how many stars there are in space.

702. A cloud of dust or gas in space is called a nebula.

703. NASA's first spacesuits were for the Mercury program.

704. There is a gigantic cloud of water vapour in space floating billions of lightyears away from Earth.

705. Uranus is the coldest planet in the Solar System, the coldest temperature recorded there was 224°C.

706. The moon has no moons and no rings.

707. A day on Venus lasts for 243 days on Earth.

708. Neptune is the most distant planet from the sun.

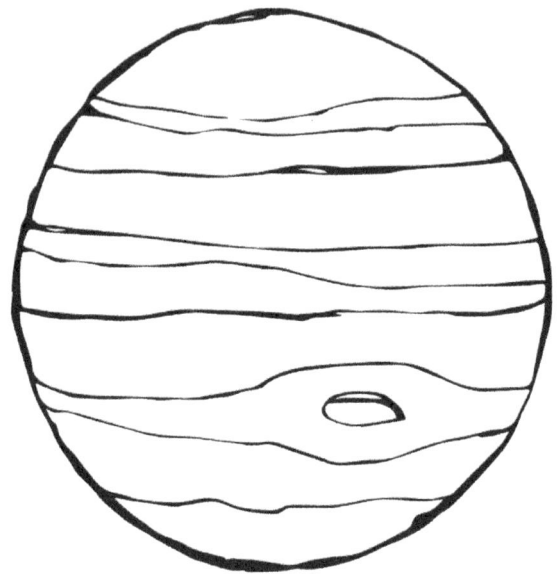

709. The Great Red Spot is a gigantic storm on the planet Jupiter.

710. There is an egg-shaped dwarf planet called Haumea beyond Neptune in the Kuiper Belt.

711. Venus spins clockwise, in the opposite direction to Earth.

712. More than 1 million Earths could fit inside the sun.

713. Astronaut's footprints on the moon could be there for a million years as there is no wind to blow them away.

714. Saturn's rings are made of orbiting ice and rock.

---

715. Mercury and Venus are the only two planets without moons.

---

716. Titan is Saturn's largest moon.

---

717. Sunsets on Mars appear blue.

---

718. Pluto has mountains, valleys, and craters.

---

719. The sun is approximately 4.6 billion years old.

---

720. There are no known planets made up of lava in the Solar System.

---

721. Mars is the second smallest planet in the Solar System.

---

722. There have been more missions to Mars than any other planet.

---

723. Venus is the brightest planet in the sky.

---

724. NASA's Voyager 2 is the only spacecraft so far to have visited Uranus.

---

725. Neptune has supersonic winds. They are the fastest winds of any planet in our Solar System.

---

726. Jupiter rotates faster than any other planet in the Solar System.

---

727. Pluto was reclassified as a dwarf planet in 2006.

---

728. Gravity keeps planets in orbit around the sun.

---

729. Thick clouds of sulfuric acid cover Venus' atmosphere.

---

730. Ganymede of Jupiter is the largest moon in the Solar System.

---

731. The distance between Earth to the sun is known as the Astronomical Unit.

---

732. No matter where you are on Earth, you will always see the same side of the moon.

---

733. Scientists know more about the moon than they do about the ocean.

---

734. Comets are made of dust, ice, and rock.

---

735. There are more trees on Earth than there are stars in the Milky Way Galaxy.

---

736. Four planets have rings, they are: Jupiter, Saturn, Neptune, and Uranus.

---

737. The first human spaceflight Voskok 1 was made by the Soviet Union in 1961.

---

738. Buzz Aldrin was the second man to walk on the moon.

---

739. Europa is a moon of Jupiter.

---

740. Olympus Mons is a huge volcano on Mars.

---

741. Mars is also known as the "Red Planet".

---

742. A dog called Laika was the first animal to orbit around the Earth on the Soviet spacecraft Sputnik 2 in 1957.

---

743. The North Star is also known as "Polaris".

---

744. There are three types of galaxies: elliptical, spiral, and irregular.

---

745. Red dwarf stars are the most common stars in the Milky Way.

---

746. Saturn is the flattest planet in the Solar System.

---

747. Mercury has the most craters of any planet in the Solar System.

---

748. Exoplanets are planets that are beyond our Solar System.

---

749. Russia's space agency is called Roskosmos.

---

750. Triton is Neptune's largest moon.

Facts about Food for Budding Foodies

751. The calcium in milk strengthens your bones.

---

752. Chickpeas are used to make hummus.

---

753. KFC stands for Kentucky Fried Chicken.

---

754. Meat, eggs, and fish are a source of protein.

---

755. Canola is an abbreviation for "Canadian oil".

---

756. Mageirocophobia is the fear of cooking.

---

757. Sailors and pirates used to suffer from scurvy. This is a disease caused by a lack of vitamin C.

---

758. When it's stored properly, honey will never go bad.

759. Pepperoni is the most popular pizza topping in the United States.

---

760. Gumbo is a stew that is popular in Louisiana, United States.

---

761. There is a Spam Museum in Austin, Minnesota, United States.

---

762. The döner kebap is one of Turkey's most famous dishes.

---

763. Carrots don't just grow to be orange in colour, they can also be purple, red, white, and yellow.

---

764. Rhubarb is a natural laxative, if you eat a bunch of rhubarb, it will make you poop.

---

765. KFC is a traditional Christmas dinner in Tokyo, Japan following a 1974 advertising campaign that said, "Kentucky is Christmas".

---

766. Spinach and Kale are high sources of iron.

---

767. Almonds (Prunus dulcis) are a member of the prunus family, this also includes peaches (Prunus persicus).

---

768. Porridge is a breakfast made by cooking oats with either milk or water.

---

769. Sheep milk is used to make cheese including feta, manchego, pecorino, and roquefort.

---

770. The spiciest curry in the world is Phaal curry.

---

771. Mexico is the biggest producer of avocados in the world.

---

772. Raisins are dry grapes.

---

773. Basil is the herb in pesto sauce.

---

774. Glamorgan sausages are not made of meat, they are made from cheese.

---

775. Basmati is a long-grain rice that is mostly grown in India, Pakistan, and Nepal.

---

776. Black pudding is made from pork or beef blood.

---

777. A Gugelhupf is a tall and creased cake with a hole in the middle of it.

---

778. Seville oranges are used to make marmalade.

---

779. Bobotie is the national dish of South Africa.

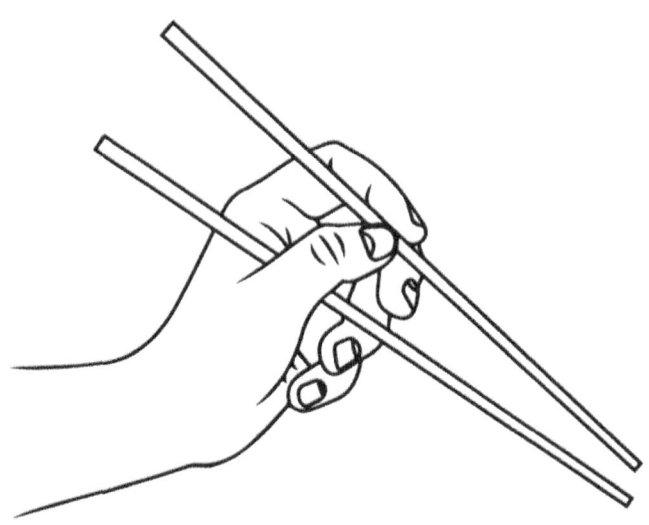

780. China produces the most chopsticks in the world.

---

781. English Toffee Day is on 8th January.

---

782. Lachanophobia is a fear of vegetables.

---

783. Escargot is from the French word for snail.

---

784. Pad Thai is a famous stir-fry noodle street food dish in Thailand.

---

785. "Sunny-side-up" is an expression that means an egg is fried on one side only.

---

786. The bubbles in fizzy drinks are caused by carbon dioxide gas.

---

787. Toad in the hole is an English dish of sausages in Yorkshire pudding batter.

---

788. Oolong is a traditional Chinese tea which is made by withering the plant under a strong sun to cause oxidation.

---

789. Chilli con carne means "chilli with meat" when it's translated from Spanish.

---

790. Bánh mì is a Vietnamese baguette filled with savoury ingredients or meat.

---

791. There is a pumpkin called the Cinderella pumpkin which looks like the one in the 1950 Disney movie.

---

792. Scallions are a type of green onion that is also called spring onions.

---

793. The most popular dish for home cooking and eating out is curry rice.

---

794. Churros are traditionally paired with chocolate dip.

---

795. Mozzarella cheese is made from buffalo milk.

---

796. The passion fruit is native to southern Brazil.

---

797. In 1834, Dr John Cook used to sell ketchup as medicine in the form of "tomato pills".

---

798. The country that drinks the most tea in the world is Turkey.

---

799. Raw lettuce has a water content of over 95%.

---

800. Mussels are mollusks that live in lakes, rivers, and creeks.

Things You Didn't Know about Science and Nature

801. The kidneys cleanse the blood of toxins and turn the waste into urine.

_____

802. Most adults have 32 teeth.

_____

803. A male cow is called an ox.

_____

804. All animals need food, air, water, and shelter to survive.

_____

805. The respiratory system is the organs and tissue that enable you to breathe.

_____

806. Seawater is saltier than the salt in our blood.

_____

807. Bees have four wings.

_____

808. The ozone layer is a shield in Earth's atmosphere that protects us from the Sun's harmful rays.

_____

809. Earth is the third planet from the sun.

_____

810. The three states of matter are solid, liquid, and gas.

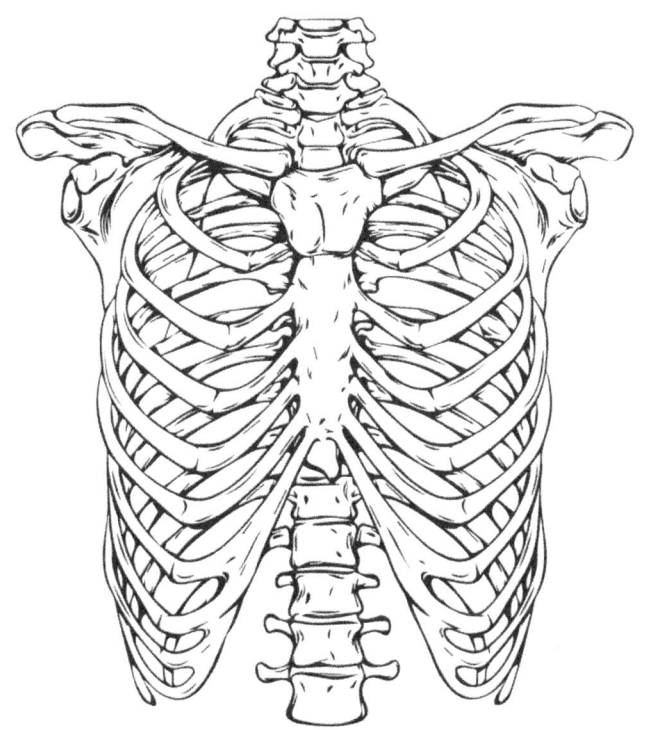

811. The rib cage protects the heart and lungs.

812. A group of moles is called a "labour".

813. The two holes in the nose are called nostrils.

814. Water covers 71% of Earth's surface.

815. Plants get minerals from soil which help them to grow.

_____

816. Temperature tells us how hot or cold something is.

_____

817. Pollen is a powder produced by the male part of the flower.

_____

818. The chemical symbol for silver is Ag.

_____

819. Plants are fixed into the soil by their roots.

_____

820. Violet is the innermost colour of a rainbow.

_____

821. An animal that belongs to the cat family is known as a feline.

_____

822. The offspring of frogs and toads are called tadpoles.

_____

823. Cats cannot taste sugar.

_____

824. The biggest animal on Earth is the blue whale.

_____

825. The boiling point of water is 100 °C or 212 °F.

_____

826. Earth Day is held on April 22nd to support environmental protection.

_____

827. Usually, the freezing point or melting point of water is 0 °C or 32 °F.

_____

828. Emeralds are green gemstones.

_____

829. The Tower of London is home to several ravens.

_____

830. Camels are known as "ships of the desert" as they can carry heavy loads from one across deserts.

_____

831. It takes approximately 365 for the Earth to orbit the sun.

_____

832. The skull protects the brain from injury.

_____

833. A material that is see-through is called "transparent".

_____

834. The cassowary is a dangerous bird that has great size and strength.

_____

835. Tendons connect muscles to bone.

_____

836. Magma is the hot liquid rock that lies beneath the Earth's surface.

---

837. The Kalahari Desert covers is in Botswana, and parts of Namibia and South Africa.

---

838. The Potomac River runs through Washington D.C.

---

839. The hyoid bone in the neck is the only bone that isn't connected to any other bone in the human body.

---

840. Littering is a type of pollution.

---

841. Dock leaves can ease the pain caused by stinging nettles.

___

842. Most cats have 18 paws.

___

843. Edelweiss is the national flower of Austria.

___

844. Talc is the softest mineral in the world.

___

845. A herbivore is an animal that eats plants.

___

846. Thermometers are used to check the temperature.

___

847. The horn of a rhino is made from keratin, not bone, this is the same material found in your hair and fingernails.

___

848. Removing a forest or trees for non-forest use is called deforestation.

___

849. The sea parrot is more commonly known as the puffin.

___

850. Angel Falls is three times taller than the Eiffel Tower in Paris, France.

___

851. Earth is the only planet in our Solar System known to support life.

---

852. The guppy or rainbow fish is one of the most popular tropical fish that you will see at an aquarium.

---

853. Dogs have a strong sense of smell due to their number of scent receptors.

---

854. An omnivore eats both plants and animals.

---

855. The silkworm caterpillar is native to China.

---

856. Giraffes only live in Africa.

---

857. Gravity is the force that keeps us on the ground.

---

858. Magnets have two poles, a north pole, and a south pole.

---

859. Spiders have eight legs.

---

860. The art of trimming and shaping shrubs or trees is known as topiary.

---

861. Air is put inside packets of crisps to stop them from getting crushed during transit.

862. The Fujita Scale or F Scale is used to measure tornadoes based on wind damage.

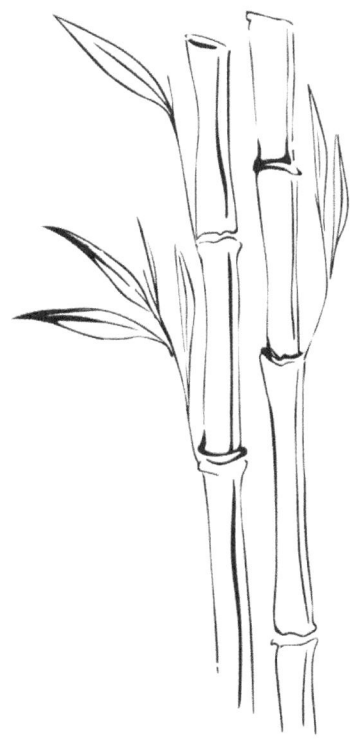

863. Giant bamboo is the tallest grass in the world.

864. The radula is the correct name for a mollusk's tongue.

865. Yeast is a type of fungus.

_____

866. A chameleon's tongue can be twice the length of its body.

_____

867. The largest known star in the universe is UY Scuti.

_____

868. Delphinus delphis is the Latin name for the common dolphin.

_____

869. Goliath beetles are the heaviest insects in the world.

_____

870. A nidologist studies birds' nests.

_____

871. Pacific Sea Wasps are extremely venomous jellyfish that live in Northern Australia.

_____

872. Anemometers are used to measure wind speed.

_____

873. Volcanoes can produce lightning at the start of an eruption.

_____

874. The iris is the coloured part of the eye.

_____

875. "Os coxae" is the proper term for the hip bone.

---

876. Bordered by Israel and Jordan, the Dead Sea has a salt content of around 34%.

---

877. A long period without rain is called a drought.

---

878. The Bermuda Triangle is in the North Atlantic Ocean.

---

879. A shad is a type of North American fish that hatch in freshwater rivers.

---

880. Saw-wort is a purple flower with narrow leaves that is a member of the daisy family.

---

881. Norway Spruce is the traditional Christmas tree that has been popular since Victorian times.

---

882. Mosquitoes have two wings.

---

883. A scaup is a type of diving duck.

---

884. Large bodies of water surrounded by land are called lakes.

---

885. Malbec is a purple grape that is famous in Bordeaux, France and Mendoza, Argentina.

---

886. Aloe Vera is a herb, it's used to treat sunburn.

---

887. A female alligator is called a cow.

---

888. Most caterpillars have 12 eyes.

---

889. Eyelashes are there to protect your eyes.

890. Bonsai is a famous type of art in Japan and China which involves sculpting miniature trees.

---

891. Apiculture is the technical term for maintaining bee colonies and beekeeping.

---

892. Antibiotics are given to fight bacterial infections, not viruses.

---

893. Bats are the only flying mammals.

---

894. The mandible or jawbone is the largest and strongest bone in the human skull.

---

895. The wren is the most common bird in the United Kingdom.

---

896. Caviar comes from sturgeon fish.

---

897. A group of dolphins is called a "pod".

---

898. Catawba is a reddish type of North American grape.

---

899. Hekla volcano is in Iceland and in the Middle Ages it was nicknamed "the Gateway to Hell".

---

900. Sea turtles don't have teeth.

A Whirlwind of General Knowledge Trivia for Geniuses

901. Julia Gillard became the first female prime minister of Australia in 2010.

---

902. Silverstone Circuit is a famous Formula 1 racecourse in Northamptonshire, England.

---

903. Superman was born on the fictional planet of Krypton and his birth name was Kal-El.

---

904. Colombo is the capital city of Sri Lanka.

---

905. Sally Ride became the first woman from the United States to fly in space in 1983.

---

906. Delaware was the first state of the modern United States of America.

---

907. There are four quarters in a dollar.

---

908. The German classical composer Ludwig van Beethoven was almost totally deaf and unable to hear by the age of 44 years old.

---

909. Kodiak Island is Alaska's biggest fishing port.

---

910. Venetian explorer and merchant Marco Polo is famous for travelling along the Silk Road between 1271 and 1295.

---

911. A pentagon has five sides.

---

912. San Francisco is in the state of California.

---

913. Chickens are curious animals and like to play with objects.

---

914. A three-wheeled bicycle is called a "tricycle".

---

915. India is in Asia.

---

916. There are six zeroes in a million.

---

917. Jupiter has the highest gravity of the planets in the Solar System.

---

918. The Phantom of the Opera is the longest-running show on Broadway, New York.

---

919. A hexagon has six sides.

___

920. Area 51 is a secret United States Air Force military base in the state of Nevada.

___

921. *"The Starry Night"* is a famous painting by Vincent van Gogh.

___

922. In the famous nursery rhyme *"Jack and Jill"*, Jack and Jill went up the hill to fetch a pale of water.

___

923. The Great Pyramid of Giza was built for Pharaoh Khufu.

___

924. There are 12 inches in a foot.

___

925. Paella is the national food dish of Spain.

___

926. The villain in *"Aladdin"* is called Jafar.

___

927. Every human has their own unique smell.

___

928. The Kosmoceratops dinosaur had 15 horns on its head.

___

929. Philadephia, Pennsylvania is known as "the City of Brotherly Love".

---

930. The technical name for salt is sodium chloride.

---

931. There are 52 weeks in a year.

---

932. Uruguay won the first-ever football FIFA World Cup in 1930.

933. A griffin is a mythological creature that has the body of a lion and wings and the head of an eagle.

---

934. Venison is this generic term for deer meat.

935. The iconic red K2 telephone box was introduced to the public of London in 1926.

936. Valentine's Day is celebrated on 14th February.

937. The Apostolic Palace, Vatican City is the official residence of the Pope.

938. The average yawn will last for approximately six seconds.

939. Sapphire is a blue gemstone.

---

940. At a latitude of -41, Wellington, New Zealand is the southernmost capital city in the world.

---

941. In the bible, David fought Goliath.

---

942. A barometer is used to measure air pressure.

---

943. The statue of Jesus, called Christ the Redeemer is in Rio de Janeiro, Brazil.

---

944. When we are scared, our vision improves.

---

945. Bad breath is also called halitosis.

---

946. Sean Connery played the first-ever James Bond on the big screen in the 1962 movie "*Dr. No*".

---

947. The Roman Baths are in Bath, England.

---

948. HTTP stands for "Hypertext Transfer Protocol".

---

949. Schiphol is the international airport of Amsterdam in the Netherlands.

---

950. The Ancient Egyptian sun god was called Ra.

---

951. World Literacy Day is celebrated on September 8th.

---

952. Henry VIII became the King of England in 1509.

---

953. Hawaii used to be called the Sandwich Islands.

---

954. Reykjavik, Iceland is the most northernly capital city in the world.

---

955. Buckingham Palace is in London, England.

---

956. In Irish mythology, a leprechaun is fairy-like and usually takes the form of an old man.

---

957. Samsung makes the Galaxy series of smartphones.

---

958. The African nation of Malawi used to be called Nyasaland.

---

959. Tooth enamel is the hardest substance in the human body.

---

960. Cambridge, England used to be known by the Romans as Duroliponte.

---

961. The Channel Tunnel links England and France.

---

962. Stephen Hawking wrote the book "*A Brief History of Time*" about the Big Bang and Black Holes.

---

963. Tweezers can be used to pluck stray eyebrow hairs.

---

964. English, Mandarin Chinese, Hindi, and Spanish are the four most spoken languages in the world.

---

965. Wrinkles around the eye are nicknamed "crow's feet".

---

966. Duffel bags are named after Duffel, a town in Antwerp, Belgium where the material was produced.

---

967. The 20th Century started on 1 January 1901.

---

968. Mahatma Gandhi's first name was actually Mohandas.

---

969. The shortcut for "copy" on a computer keyboard is "Ctrl + C".

---

970. A giraffe has seven neckbones.

---

971. A fern leaf is called a frond.

---

972. Jamaica is the third-largest island in the Caribbean.

---

973. Tokyo used to be called Edo, the name was changed in 1868.

---

974. The Premier League of English football was founded on 27 May 1992.

---

975. Bram Stoker is the author of the horror story *"Dracula"*.

---

976. Canis lupus is the scientific name for a wolf.

---

977. The Transantarctic Mountains are in Antarctica.

---

978. Rolex watches have a pointed crown on their logo.

---

979. The Dutch eat oliebollen (fried doughnuts) on New Year's Eve.

---

980. Solar flares are violent explosions in the Sun's atmosphere.

---

981. The International Space Station (ISS) follows the time zone of Greenwich Mean Time (GMT) on Earth.

---

982. Gingivitis is a common gum disease.

---

983. Methane is generated by decay in marshes and bogs. It's also called Marsh gas.

---

984. Stretching exercises help to improve your flexibility.

---

985. Crackers are bad for your teeth as they can get lodged in them.

---

986. Hebrew is the official language of Israel.

---

987. Cats "meow" at humans to communicate something.

---

988. There is a part of Canada that is south of Detroit, United States.

---

989. Orcas are not whales, they are a type of dolphin.

---

990. The Sea of Tranquility is located on the Moon.

---

991. A falchion is a type of curved sword.

---

992. The first episode of *"The Simpsons"* aired on 17 December 1989.

---

993. The US Masters golf tournament is held at the Augusta National Golf Club.

---

994. Surfing is a popular sport of Bondi Beach in Sydney, Australia.

995. In Chess, a Bishop can only move diagonally.

996. The colour green means "GO" on traffic lights.

997. Insects don't have lungs.

998. Norwegian is the spoken language in Norway.

999. A baker's dozen means there are 13 of something.

1000. Crete is the largest Greek island.

Conclusion

Alas, we have finally reached the end of our fact-finding journey wandering through some of the strangest and most amazing realities and trivia that make Earth the greatest planet in the whole universe.

On the road we have time-travelled all the way back to Ancient Egypt and Abraham Lincoln's America. Our voyage has also explored Earth's oceans to the outer-most depths of space.

We've encountered astronauts and Olympic gold medalists, presidents and kings, blue whales and dinosaurs—and even spent some time marveling at the magnitude of the pyramids.

I addition to having fun and getting some enjoyment out of this book, you have most certainly learned a thing or two, not just about some specific facts about individuals but about the entire world.

By now you should be armed with lots of new mind-blowing facts and stories to tell your friends at school or to use at your next trivia night. And remember, the next time you see or hear about something totally crazy or wonderous, know that it may make future volumes of this book.

If you've been with us since page one—would you please be so kind as to leave a rating with your thoughts on the book?

Until next time!

MORE BOOKS BY HENRY BENNETT...

I hope you enjoyed this book and learned something new. Please check out some of my other publications.

Dive into...

THE
UNBELIEVABLE
FACTS
BOOK

Hilariously Weird Facts & Fascinating
Stories from Planet Earth

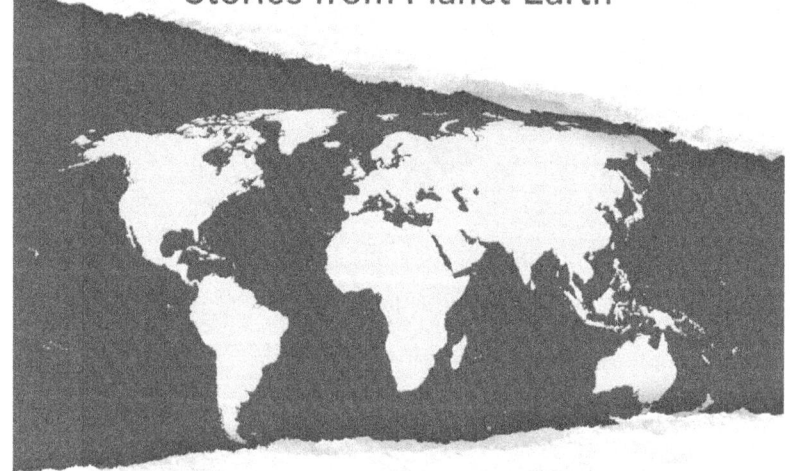

HENRY BENNETT

DON'T FORGET YOUR BONUS BOOKS!

To help you along your investing in knowledge journey, we've provided a free and exclusive copy of the short book, *Amazing Quick-Fire Facts,* and a bonus copy of book, *The Big Book of Fun Riddles & Jokes.*

We highly recommend you sign up now to get the most out of these books. You can do that by visiting https://www.subscribepage.com/henrybennett to receive your FREE copies!

Bibliography

Britannica.com. (2022). *Britannica* (online). https://www.britannica.com/

Businessinsider.com. (2022). *Businessinsider* (online). https://www.businessinsider.com/

Chemicool.com. (2022). *Chemicool* (online). https://www.chemicool.com/

Chess.com. (2022). *Chess.com* (online). https://www.chess.com/

Chicagotribune.com. (2022). *Chicago Tribune* (online). https://www.chicagotribune.com/

Climatekids.nasa.gov (2022). *NASA Climate Kids* (online). https://climatekids.nasa.gov/

Coca-colacompany.com. (2022). *The Coca-Company* (online). https://www.coca-colacompany.com/

Cosmopolitan.com. (2022). *Cosmopolitan* (online). https://www.cosmopolitan.com/

Dictionary.com. (2022). *Dictionary.com* (online). https://www.dictionary.com/

Foodnetwork.co.uk. (2022). *Food Network* (online). https://foodnetwork.co.uk/

Grammarhow.com. (2022). *Grammar How* (online). https://grammarhow.com/

Guinnessworldrecords.com. (2022). *Guinness World Records* (online). https://www.guinnessworldrecords.com/

Harpercollins.com. (2022). *Harper Collins* (online). https://www.harpercollins.com/

Healthline.com. (2022). *Health Line* (online). https://www.healthline.com/

Historyhit.com. (2022). *History Hit* (online). https://www.historyhit.com/

Hopkinsmedicine (2022). *John Hopkins Medicine* (online). https://www.hopkinsmedicine.org/

Legolanddiscoverycentre.com. (2022). Legoland Discovery Centre (online). https://www.legolanddiscoverycentre.com/

Losangelestimes.com. (2022). *Los Angeles Times* (online). https://www.latimes.com/

Msa.maryland.gov. (2002). *Maryland (*online). https://msa.maryland.gov/

Nasa.gov. (2022). *NASA* (online). https://www.nasa.gov/

Nassauparadiseisland.com. (2022). *Nassau Paradise Island* (online). https://www.nassauparadiseisland.com/

Natgeokids.com. (2022). *National Geographic Kids* (online). https://www.natgeokids.com/

Nationalgeographic.com. (2022). *National Geographic* (online). https://www.nationalgeographic.com/

NFSA.gov.au. (2022). *National Film and Sound Archive of Australia* (online). https://www.nfsa.gov.au/

Oceanservice.noaa.gov. (2022). *National Ocean Service* (online). https://oceanservice.noaa.gov/

Olympics.com. (2022). *Olympics* (online). https://olympics.com/

Pekkeen.com. (2022). *Pet Keen* (online). https://petkeen.com/

Sciencefocus.com. (2022). *Science Focus* (online). https://www.sciencefocus.com/

Sciencekids.co.nz. (2022). *Science Kid* (online). https://www.sciencekids.co.nz/

Ship-technology.com. (2022). *Ship Technology* (online). https://www.ship-technology.com/

Space-facts.com. (2022). *Space Facts* (online). https://space-facts.com/

Thenewyorktimes.com. (2022). *The New York Times* (online). https://www.nytimes.com/

Visitnorway.com. (2022). *Norway* (online). https://www.visitnorway.com/

Vocabulary.com. (2022). *Vocabulary.com* (online). https://www.vocabulary.com/

Whc.unesco.org. (2022). *UNESCO World Heritage Convention* (online). https://whc.unesco.org/

Yahoo.com. (2022). *Yahoo* (online). www.yahoo.com/

Made in the USA
Monee, IL
02 December 2022

19422399R00094